# The Nuts and Bolts of Bible Prophecy

# Core Teachings Explained

ERIKA GREY

Pedante Press

Short Book Series

002

Copyright © 2020 Erika Grey

All rights reserved.

Special Thanks to Jerri O'Roke who proofread and edited this work.

ISBN: 978-1-940844-14-5

## DEDICATION

To my father who made this work possible.

# CONTENTS

|    | Acknowledgments | i |
|----|-----------------|---|
| 1  | End Times Bible Prophecy | 1 |
| 2  | Prophecy Topics | 5 |
| 3  | Signs of the End Times | 11 |
| 4  | Rapture of the Church | 15 |
| 5  | The Tribulation | 25 |
| 6  | Antichrist | 33 |
| 7  | Beast of Revelation | 37 |
| 8  | Mark of the Beast | 45 |
| 9  | Whore of Babylon | 48 |
| 10 | Revelation | 53 |
| 11 | Bible Prophecy News | 61 |

**www.erikagrey.com**

For Bible Prophecy news and analysis and more books visit my website. For Bible Prophecy Updates on video subscribe to my YouTube channel Prophecy Talk with Erika Grey.

# 1 END TIMES BIBLE PROPHECY

One-third of the Bible's message is prophetic. There are sixty-six books of the Bible. Thirty-nine of these make up what is called the Old Testament. These books are divided into the Pentateuch (the first five books of the Old Testament), twelve historical books, five poetic, and seventeen prophetic. The books of the prophets fall under one of two categories: Major or Minor Prophets. The New Testament has twenty-seven texts. These also include historical books. In addition, there are the Pauline epistles (those written by the Apostle Paul), non-Pauline epistles, and one prophetic book. The Revelation—the last book of the Bible—predicts the end of the world events.

All Prophecy has already been fulfilled, with the exception of those pertaining to the earth's final years recorded in the Revelation. The signs, which Jesus predicted would lead up to those final days, Evangelicals refer to as "end times prophecy."

## The Biblical Books With End Times Forecasts

The chief books for end times prophecy are the Revelation and the book of Daniel. Additionally, Jesus's predictions of the last days found in the Gospels add more details. Prophetic passages also lie within the Major and Minor Prophets. Biblical books such as Genesis, the Psalms, Thessalonians, and 2 Timothy have various verses that provide more specifics to the end times prophecies recorded in the major prophetic books.

## What is The Study of End Times Prophecy?

During Jesus's ministry, people questioned him about the end of time on earth. Jesus foretold the signs that will lead to His second coming. He described life just before and during the Tribulation. In summary, the study of end times prophecy is the study of the earth's final seven years of Tribulation and the decades leading up to the fulfillment of what Jesus predicted for those years.

## How Does One Study End Times Prophecy?

It is important to understand the books of the Bible before you begin to study end times prophecy and/or Bible Prophecy. Familiarize yourself with the books of the Bible as a whole. From there, become knowledgeable with the various teachings of end times prophecy. Consult theologians, a Bible dictionary, and a good online concordance. Be prepared to spend a good deal of time doing your research and study.

Furthermore, if you will relate the forecasts to world affairs, you will need to possess more than a basic knowledge of events. Finally, make sure the websites that you obtain your information on world affairs are from top-of-the-line sources. Consequently, many inaccuracies are taught because of lack of reading quality news outlets. Simply put, consult websites like Prophecy Talk. My site is filled with a good deal of information that meets all of the above criteria.

Whatever you do, be on guard against the many false teachings. Moreover, stay clear of conspiracy theories and the One World Government, New World Order cults. Their teachings on current affairs are fake news, lies, and far removed from reality.

Information is available as never before. The speed in which to access that information has significantly increased. No longer do you have to flip through the pages of a Concordance. With the click of a mouse, you can obtain its contents literally right at your fingertips. These—along with Bible Dictionaries and Commentaries—are found online. In studying the Bible and world affairs, the larger issue is knowing where to find the key facts.

# 2 PROPHECY TOPICS

Within the Bible, key end times Prophecy teachings and topics emerge. Many teachers mark their starting point with the signs of the times that Jesus predicted.

Among all who teach end times prophecy, there are common key terms, and these are among those listed below. Some are written as subcategories.

**The Three Types of End Times Prophecy Terms or Topics**

There are two types of end times prophecy topics. They are either identified in the Bible or penned from teachings in Scripture. An example of a Biblical topic cited in Scripture is "the Antichrist." Examples of the terms taken from the Bible—versus the ones penned by Scholars—are listed below.

**Biblical Terms**

- **Antichrist**–used once in the Bible, taken from one verse.
- **Tribulation**–not named so in the Bible, but taken from Jesus's statement, "There will be great tribulation."
- **Great Tribulation**–Jesus's reference and an Elder's in the book of Revelation.
- **Abomination of Desolation**–spoken of in the book of Daniel and referenced by Jesus.
- **Whore of Babylon**–named in Revelation 17 and 18.
- **Mark of the Beast**–labeled in the book of Revelation.

**Non-Biblical Terms for End Times Prophecy Teachings**

- **Rapture**–derived from Biblical description.

- **Tribulation**–Seven_ —year period of judgements.
- **Peace Treaty**–covenant agreed to by Antichrist on behalf of Israel.
- **Final World Empire**–Daniel's fourth kingdom that ushers in the end.
- **Unholy Trinity**–represents Satan, Antichrist, and the False Prophet

## Speculative Terms

Some of the speculative terms listed below are now dated. In addition, cult like teachings and conspiracy theories have resulted. Avoid giving these any major focus in your studies.

New World Order
One World Religion
One World Government

I, personally, have not found evidence in Scripture of a one world religion; moreover, an empire with world rule applies better than a one world government.

The above list is not exhaustive, but it demonstrates three categories of terms for end times Bible Prophecy topics.

## The above terms are overused clichés

Again, a word of caution on the topics. These terms have become clichés that have no basis in geopolitics. For instance, teachers will include one world government and one world religion within their instructions. In the case of one world government, it is largely overused and abused in Evangelical circles.

In addition, it is used by the New World Order cult within prophecy circles. This cult teaches that the UN is a government—which is not true. It is far removed from how the UN and world works. These groups rely on lies and emotions, instead of facts, to get their message across. Their message is dangerous because it negates the power of prophecy in the eyes of the world.

New World Order is also used to mean the setup of the conspiratorial governments. It is another end time cliché. We are in what is called a multi-polar era—or empire age. This lines 100% with the book of Daniel's and Revelation's forecast.

As I stated earlier, I see no evidence in Scripture of a one world religion. This term means that all of the religions of the world will form into one unified group at the time of the end. Therefore, in the absence of evidence, I do not teach this.

## Many differences exist in the study of end times prophecy

While many differences exist in the speculation of world affairs, there are also those that exist among key teachings. The greatest area of disagreement concerning end times prophecy is the topic of the Rapture. Some teachers disagree that the Bible predicts a Rapture. Others who do agree dispute its timing. Some say the Rapture occurs pretribulation, others mid tribulation or post tribulation.

Other areas of discord regard the identity of the four beasts in Daniel and the Beast of Revelation. In addition, there are disagreements to the description and origin of the Antichrist.

The main area of opposing teachings in end times prophecy peaks in the speculation of the prophetic forecasts to current world news. In this area arises all kinds of false, fictitious and cult like teachings that dominate the airwaves.

Search engines are another tool of deception. When one types in a prophecy term, the Cult websites dominate many of the first pages.

**Key End Times Prophecy Biblical Topics**

Within the study of end time forecasts are key topics that all interrelate. We will be covering each of them and their subtopics. They are as follows:

- End Time Signs – the birth pangs, the fig tree
- The Rapture
- The Tribulation and Great Tribulation
- The Antichrist
- The Beast of Revelation – the revived Roman empire – the final world empire – Nebuchadnezzar's dream image – Seven to eight heads on Beast of Revelation
- Mark of the Beast – image of the Beast – the False Prophet
- Whore of Babylon – Judgement of the Great Whore – Destruction of Babylon
- Book of Revelation plagues – the four horsemen of the apocalypse – the 144 thousand witnesses – the two witnesses

–the battle of Armageddon – the 200 million man army – the spirits like frogs– Bowl Judgments – seven trumpets – three woes – angel from the bottomless pit: Apollyon. These are among the many topics found in the Revelation.
- Israel – The peace treaty and the Third Temple – the abomination of desolation.

Note: This is not an exhaustive list and there are more topics. This book provides an overview of the most discussed and—as the title states—the nuts and bolts of Bible Prophecy.

# 3 SIGNS OF THE END TIMES

During Jesus's ministry, the disciples asked Him about the end of the world. Jesus told them about the signs what would lead to His second coming. These would consist of markers in nature and society. They are primarily found in the following passages:

Matthew 24
Mark 13
2 Timothy 3:1-5
2 Peter 3

1 Timothy 4:1-3
Revelation 13
Daniel 12:4
Revelation 13:18
Revelation 17

Several of the end times passages reveal the evils in society that grow to unforeseen heights before the start of the Tribulation. Jesus compared their intensity to the birth pangs of a woman in labor. He also likened the events both social and political to the fig tree with budding fruit.

Those who understand the times will know when the tree is about to produce its bounty. According to Jesus's prediction, we will see an increase in the following areas in line with the birth pangs of a woman in labor.

- Wars
- Violence – brutality – a loveless society
- Riots – commotions
- Pestilences and plagues – illnesses and insects
- Natural disasters
- Strange occurrences in nature
- Sexual immorality
- Lawlessness

- Increased sinfulness in all areas — e.g., greed, gluttony, addiction, etc.

2 Timothy 3: 1-5 summed up the last days as being perilous because of the evil that will prevail in society. The passage uses such terms as "brutal," "unloving," and "lovers of themselves" to describe men during that time.

Daniel 8:23 defines it as "when the transgressors are come to the full," meaning that society will get extremely wicked.

# 4 THE RAPTURE

The Rapture is a term that Evangelical Christians have given to the teaching that those who are redeemed by the blood of Jesus will not go through the Tribulation. Therefore, they will be taken out of the earth just before the Tribulation begins and meet the Lord in the sky. Those living prior to the Rapture will have lived through the fulfillment of the end times with all the hardships they bring.

## Is the term Rapture used in the Bible?

The term Rapture of the church is not used in the Bible. It is a term and teaching first noted and taught by British theologian and Bible translator, John Nelson Darby, in around 1830.

Darby is the father of dispensationalism. In his day, he was the leading interpreter of Biblical Prophecy.

**The Rapture of the Church is one of the most disputed topics in end time Bible Prophecy**

Evangelical Christians are divided on their interpretation of the Rapture Scriptures. Some believe the Rapture occurs after the Tribulation. Others trust it happens before the Tribulation begins. Then there are those who believe that it never takes place.

Based on my analysis of the Scriptures, I take the view that the Rapture will occur prior to the start of the Tribulation. Jesus clearly describes two distinct and diverse settings that sets apart His coming for believers in the Rapture. Details of His second coming provide an opposing description.

**The Rapture of the Church has given way to several theological terms**

The terms for the Rapture's views are pre, mid, and post Tribulation. Pretribulation means that believers meet Christ in the air before the

Tribulation begins. Those who adhere to the mid-tribulation viewpoint advocate that believers will go through part of the Tribulation; however, they will escape the Great Tribulation—the last three and one-half years. The post-tribulation position espouses that Christ comes only at the end of the Tribulation. Consequently, this topic is so disputed that there exists the Pre-Trib Research Center (PTRC). Therefore, for the sake of clarity, I am going to make clear that this work holds a pre-tribulation view—mostly because of my own research on the topic.

## The Rapture is the hope for believers who are living in the end times

The teaching of the Rapture is based on several Bible passages. In addition, God's pattern at the time of the destruction of Sodom and Gomorrah and during the flood demonstrates the removal of the righteous. They did not go through the judgments—God gave them a way out beforehand.

God Himself stated to Abraham before the obliteration of Sodom and Gomorrah that if there were ten righteous within the city, He would not annihilate it. We see the same pattern during the Tribulation regarding the Tribulation saints. The worst of the plagues occur in the final 30 days after the Antichrist's regime murders the last Christian. Moreover, the final plagues occur in response to the killing of the righteous.

Revelation 16:3-6 records the unleashing of waters turning to blood plagues. It declares:

And I heard the angel of the waters saying, "You are righteous, O Lord, The One who is and who was and who is to be. Because You have judged these things. For they have shed the blood of saints and prophets, and you have given them blood to drink. For it is their just due."

The teaching that one will not go through the severe judgments that will occur during the Tribulation is the hope of the believer living in the end times.

**Key Rapture Verses and Passages**

The Rapture teaching derives from specific passages in the Bible. In these verses we find opposite teachings of what is taught at Christ's coming at the end of the Tribulation.

## We shall not all sleep

1 Corinthians 15:51-52 states, "Behold, I tell you a mystery: We shall not all sleep, but we shall all be changed—in a moment, in the twinkling of an eye, at the last trumpet. For the trumpet will sound, and the dead will be raised incorruptible, and we shall be changed."

The key phrase in the above verse is "we shall not all sleep." Sleep in the Bible refers to death. "We shall not all sleep" means that some will not experience a physical death. In contrast, the Bible teaches death awaits the Saints living during the Tribulation.

The books of Daniel and the Revelation are very specific in that the Antichrist and his regime will martyr the Saints. This prophecy specifies a 1260 day—or a three-and-one-half-year—time frame, starting with the abomination of desolation, when these murders will occur. Not a single Christian will remain alive when the angels unleash the final Revelation plagues. These plagues include water turning to blood, a scorching sun, and loathsome boils on those who take the mark.

In addition, the battle of Armageddon and final destruction of the earth occurs.

**Then we who are alive**

1 Thessalonians 4:15-18 reiterates the message of 1 Corinthians 15 that we shall not all sleep or die. It addresses the subject: "…Then we who are alive…" It reads:

"For this we say to you by the word of the Lord, that we who are alive and remain until the coming of the Lord will by no means precede those who are asleep. For the Lord Himself will descend from heaven with a shout, with the voice of an archangel, and with the trumpet of God. And the dead in Christ will rise first. Then we who are alive and remain shall be caught up together with them in the clouds to meet the Lord in the air. And thus we shall always be with the Lord. Therefore comfort one another with these words."

Again, no Christians will be alive at the end of the Tribulation when Christ returns. Furthermore, Revelation 19:14 tells us that an army accompanies Christ that bears the same description as the Saints. It states, "And the armies in heaven, clothed in fine linen, white and clean, followed him upon white horses."

## These are they who come out of the Great Tribulation

In Revelation 7:9-17 John sees a great multitude that no one could number. They are from all different cultures, nations, and peoples. They stand before the throne and the Lamb clothed in white robes and singing praises to Him. Then one of the elders asked John, "Who are these arrayed in white robes, and where did they come from?"

This is a rhetorical question posed to John and he answers, "Sir you know." The rhetorical question is used to emphasize the point. He answers, "These are the ones who come out of the great tribulation, and washed their robes and made them white in the blood of the lamb. Therefore, they are before the throne of God, and serve Him day and night in His temple. And He who sits on the throne will dwell among them."

Notice the word "come out" is used, not came out, indicating present tense.

## More on the phrase "come out"

The word in the Geek for "come" is erchomai. According to *Blue letter Bible's Greek Lexicon*, the word is a "Middle voice of a primary verb used only in the present and imperfect tenses..."

The word means: to come, of persons, to come from one place to another, and used both of persons arriving and of those returning, to appear, make one's appearance, come before the public metaph. to come into being, arise, come forth, show itself, find place or influence, be established, become known, to come (fall) into or unto, to go, to follow one.

The word "come out" summaries the Rapture teaching. Hence, believers will instantly meet with Christ in the air and come out of the great Tribulation.

## Many details given for Tribulation and the Rapture

The Bible is like a treasure. The more you dig, the more you discover its wealth. The details the Bible provides and forecasts for the end times are right there. The Bible does not give vague references, but rather they are highly detailed. The more you examine, the more you find. Such is the case with the Rapture.

Missed by many are the differing details concerning Jesus's second coming versus the Rapture. Both are obviously set in different time periods and under diverse circumstances. One such verses describes two women grinding at the mill—one is left behind during a peaceful time. Another describes men hiding for fear in the clefts of rocks during the Tribulation at Christ's second coming. Jesus is depicted as coming as a Thief at the Rapture; during His second coming, He comes as the King of Kings and Lord of Lords.

## The Tribulation Dispensation

Jesus teaches perseverance and that "he who endures to the end will be saved," Matthew 24:13. The beginning of the Tribulation ends the Age of Grace. In addition, the Tribulation focuses on Israel. The remaining seven years that complete Daniel's 490 years of prophecies dealing with the sin of the nation makes this point clear.

During the Tribulation, if you take the mark of the Beast, you will lose your salvation. By taking the mark, you blaspheme the Holy Spirit. This is the abomination that makes desolate. This also supports the teaching that the removal of the Age of Grace for believers is at the start of the Tribulation.

## Finally, How Will the Rapture Occur?

This is another area that Evangelicals have speculated on because a sudden disappearance of multitudes of people sounds so farfetched. God works through the natural order of events. When He performs miracles, signs in nature accompany his works. We see this with the thundering and lightning coming from His Temple. When Jesus died on the cross, there was a great earthquake and the sun darkened. In these end times, we have entered an era of strange weather occurrences. New terms have entered our vocabulary as a result. Most likely a major atmospheric event will occur along with Christ's entrance. Scientists will attribute the atmospheric or weather event to the mass disappearances.

# 5 THE TRIBULATION

The Tribulation is the time period that the judgments detailed in the Revelation are unleashed onto the earth. The Bible specifies it occurs during a seven-year time frame. These judgments lead to the battle of Armageddon and the end of the world. The Tribulation divides into two halves. Scholars have named the second half "the Great Tribulation" because during this period, the angels release the worst of the Revelation plagues.

## Named by Jesus

The Tribulation is a term coined by Evangelical Christians for the earth's final years. It originated from Jesus's description in Mark

13:19 where He states, "For in those days there will be tribulation, such as has not been since the beginning of the creation which God created until this time, nor ever shall be.

Matthew reiterates in Matthew 24:29 Jesus's words, "Immediately after the tribulation of those days the sun will be darkened, and the moon will not give its light; the stars will fall from heaven, and the powers of the heavens will be shaken."

In Mark 13:24-26 Jesus states, "But in those days, after that tribulation, the sun will be darkened, and the moon will not give its light; the stars of heaven will fall, and the powers in the heavens will be shaken. Then they will see the Son of Man coming in the clouds with great power and glory."

## Great Tribulation Named by Jesus and in the book of Revelation

In Matthew 24:21 Jesus differentiated the Tribulation from the Great Tribulation after warning about the abomination of desolation. He warns the Jews that when that time occurs—they should flee. He states in Matthew 24:17-20:

"Let him who is on the housetop not go down and take anything out of his house. And let him who is in the field not go back to get his clothes. But woe to those who are pregnant and to those who are nursing babies in those days! And pray that your flight may not be in winter or on the Sabbath." He concludes with, "For then there will be great tribulation, such as has not been since the beginning of the world until this time, no, nor ever shall be."

## The Elder in Revelation 7:14 refers to the time period of judgements as the Great Tribulation

When John saw the multitude of people in white robes worshipping before the throne, the Elder asked him who the people were in a rhetorical question. The Elder answered him saying, "These are the ones who come out of the great tribulation." In Revelation 7:14, the Elder—like Jesus—named the entire time period as the "Great Tribulation".

## The Great Tribulation

The Great Tribulation is the second half or the last three and one-half years of the Tribulation.

Evangelicals customarily refer to it as the Great Tribulation. In the books of Daniel and the Revelation, the number of days for the final three and a half years is 1260.

The final judgements unleashed onto the earth are the most catastrophic. The Bible records the finale as "the day of the Lord." Joel describes it along with details given by Jesus and the prophets. We also find additional specifics given in the epistles and many in the Revelation. As the actions by the Antichrist signal the start of the Tribulation; they also begin the Great Tribulation. It is marked by what the prophet Daniel and Jesus describe as the "abomination of desolation."

## The Abomination of Desolation

The prophet Daniel and Jesus both forecast the abomination of desolation. It occurs when the Antichrist goes into the Holy of Holy's of the Third Temple, declares himself as God, and lays siege to Jerusalem. His army surrounds Jerusalem and he seeks to kill all Jews, Christians, and anyone adhering to any religion.

In this time frame, the Antichrist institutes the mark of the Beast. Thus, the Great Tribulation begins. The Antichrist wages war against believers—those who do not take the mark of the beast. Jesus quoted the prophet Daniel and elaborated on the event. From the abomination of desolation, the books of Daniel and the Revelation specify that 1260 days—or three and a half years—will be the time frame of the Antichrist's murderous campaign on the Saints. Each number of the number of days added together totals nine, the number for spiritual war in the Bible.

## What Occurs Prior to the Abomination of Desolation?

In the first half of the Tribulation, the Antichrist raises the European Union—the final world empire—to its pinnacle of power. The EU becomes extremely powerful under his leadership. During this time, he will have access to new technologies and will have been working on the mark of the Beast. Meanwhile, the angels will unleash the various Revelation plagues.

## The Revelation Plagues

Below is a list of plagues that will occur during the Tribulation, with the worst happening during the Great Tribulation.

• Nation rises against nation in war (Matthew 24:7). Also referred to in the battle of Armageddon and Antichrist's conquests.
• An army of 200 million slays a third of the earth's population (Revelation 9:13-21).
• A great volcanic eruption destroys a third of all sea life (Revelation 8:8)
• Hail and fire mingled with blood burns a third of all trees and grass (Revelation.8:7).
• A great star falls from heaven, poisoning a third of the earth's waters (Revelation 8:10-11).
• Day and night reverse (Revelation 8:12).
• A five-month plague of locusts stinging like scorpions leave men in agonizing pain (Revelation 9:3-5)
• Large hailstones rain down on the earth (Revelation 16:21).

## The final judgements—which occur after the Antichrist martyrs the last Christian

• Rivers, seas, and lakes become as blood, and all sea and aquatic life disappear (Revelation

16:3-4).
• The sun becomes extremely hot, and scorches men with great fear and fire (Revelation 16:8).
• Darkness fills the seat of the kingdom of the Beast, and grievous sores torment the individuals who bear the mark of the Beast (Revelation 16:2,10).
• The river Euphrates dries up, making way for the kings of the East (Revelation 16:12).

## The Tribulation Dispensation

Jesus teaches of perseverance and proclaims that "he who endures to the end will be saved." The reason is because the beginning of the Tribulation ends the age of Grace. During the Tribulation—if you take the mark of the Beast— you will lose any chance of salvation. You do not lose your salvation during the "Age of Grace" if you have been "saved by grace." When the Tribulation begins—the Age of Grace ends.

As I stated earlier, the Tribulation focuses on Israel. The remaining seven years complete Daniel's 490-year prophecy concerning Israel.

The way to achieve salvation during the Tribulation is by not taking the mark of the beast and accepting Christ as your savior. By taking the mark, you will blaspheme the Holy Spirit. This is the abomination that makes desolate. Most noteworthy, this also supports why you can lose your salvation during the Tribulation. Blasphemy of the Holy Spirit is the unpardonable sin.

## Other Details Particular to this Dispensation

During the Tribulation, the Third Temple will have significance—possibly the same that Jesus held for it during His ministry on earth. The two witnesses sent by God will perform miracles, which will be more commonplace. Therefore, Jesus warns against believing the false Christs who can also perform signs and wonders. In addition, there will be 144 thousand witnesses or evangelists who will be preaching during the Tribulation dispensation.

# 6 THE ANTICHRIST

The Antichrist evokes fear in all who first learn of him—He is the Son of Satan. The Antichrist is a leading figure in the Unholy Trinity. The Antichrist is the only man the Bible assigns a number for a name. His number is the frightful 666 combination. Hence, the triple six represents the Unholy Trinity—and a curse.

Furthermore, the Bible gives over 30 titles to him and references the Antichrist as early as Genesis. He is Jesus Christ's nemesis. Throughout Scripture we see contrast after contrast between God and the Devil, and Jesus and the Antichrist. Bible Prophecy provides the best depiction of the battle of the ages between God and Satan.

## The early church fathers wrote about him

The Old Testament prophets forecast the Antichrist. Jesus made mention of him and later the apostles referenced him. The early church fathers contributed their own writings. These included Polycarp, a disciple of John, Irenaeus, a student of Polycarp, Hippolytus who learned under Irenaeus, and Justin the Martyr. They all taught on the Antichrist's person and of his coming.

The title Antichrist is used only once in the Scriptures; yet, there are over 30 forecasts of him in the Old and New Testament.

## The Antichrist is end times Bible Prophecy's most central figure

Referred to as the man of sin, this dictator initiates the beginning of the Tribulation.

It begins when he negotiates a peace treaty with Israel; this treaty will mimic the Abrahamic covenant. Rising from the Revived Roman Empire (the European Union), he leads it into its pinnacle of power. Hence, under the Antichrist's leadership, the EU will become the greatest and strongest world power to have ever existed.

Midway during the Tribulation period—after the Antichrist has risen the EU to its pinnacle of power—he enters the Holy of Holies in the Third Temple. There he declares himself as God, and he also places the abomination of desolation.

## Antichrist's actions mark the beginning of the Great Tribulation

The Antichrist's actions divide the Tribulation into its two periods. At the start of the Great Tribulation, he lays siege to Jerusalem and institutes the image and mark of the Beast.

A figure—who the Bible refers to as a False Prophet—has an image of the Beast erected. He performs a miracle and causes the image of the Beast to speak (Revelation 13:15). Consequently, "he causes all, both small and great, rich and poor, free and slave, to take the mark of the Beast" (Revelation 13:16). The Antichrist will launch a murderous campaign against the people of God, and anyone who will not take the mark. In addition, he will abolish all religions. His actions during the Great Tribulation cause profound human suffering. In his finale, he conquers nation after nation—seeking to annihilate as many people as he can.

## The Antichrist ignites the Battle of Armageddon

One fourth of the world's population will die due to the Antichrist's policies and conquests. In addition to the suffering caused by the Antichrist, God unleashes His trumpet and bowl judgments onto the world. This is the reason for this time period being referred to as "the Great Tribulation." Finally, the Antichrist's actions usher in the battle of Armageddon.

The Antichrist is part of God's judgements. Armageddon is followed by the second coming of the Lord Jesus Christ and the end of the world.

# 7 THE BEAST OF REVELATION

**The Beast of Revelation is the final world empire (government) the Antichrist leads**

Bible Prophecy describes the Beast in both the book of Daniel and the Revelation. The major prophets provide additional details. The Beast of Revelation will become the most powerful empire to have ever existed in all of history. In the Revelation, it is described as rising from the sea. The dragon like red Beast emerges with seven to eight heads and ten horns.

The Beast roars with the mouth of a lion. The Bible depicts the Beast appearing with the strongest features of ferocious animals of prey, representing the Beast's frightful power.

Daniel 7:7 provides a horrific description of the Beast possessing monstrous, almost surreal, features. Daniel describes the Beast as being dreadful and terrible, exceedingly strong. Its lion like mouth has great iron teeth. The Beast is so powerful it both devours and destroys everything in its path. The verse describes it as breaking into pieces and trampling the residue with its feet. It states:

"After this I saw in the night visions, and behold, a fourth beast, dreadful and terrible, exceedingly strong. It had huge iron teeth; it was devouring, breaking in pieces, and trampling the residue with its feet. It was different from all the beasts that were before it, and it had ten horns."

## Daniel's Disturbing Vision

Daniel's vision greatly troubled him, and when inquiring about the fourth beast—the final world empire—he adds another detail. Not only were its teeth of iron, but its nails are of bronze. It is partially made of metal. He reiterates the beast devouring, breaking in pieces and trampling the residue under is feet.

Daniel 7:15-19 states:

"I, Daniel, was grieved in my spirit within my body, and the visions of my head troubled me. I came near to one of those who stood by, and asked him the truth of all this. So he told me and made known to me the interpretation of these things: 'Those great beasts, which are four, are four kings which arise out of the earth. But the saints of the Most High shall receive the kingdom, and possess the kingdom forever, even forever and ever.' "

"Then I wished to know the truth about the fourth beast, which was different from all the others, exceedingly dreadful, with its teeth of iron and its nails of bronze, which devoured, broke in pieces, and trampled the residue with its feet."

## The Beast's Description

Daniel 7:23 provides the meaning of the symbolism of the animals that are the fourth beast, it states:

"Thus, he said: 'The fourth beast shall be [a] fourth kingdom on earth, Which shall be different from all other kingdoms, And shall devour the whole earth, Trample it and break it in pieces.' "

In Nebuchadnezzar's dream image, we see the first picture of the final world empire. Nebuchadnezzar, king of Babylon, had a dream which he asked Daniel to interpret. It is made of iron and possesses the strength of previous empires also depicted by various metals. Daniel 2:39-40 states:

"But after you shall arise another kingdom inferior to yours; then another, a third kingdom of bronze, which shall rule over all the earth. And the fourth kingdom shall be as strong as iron, inasmuch as iron breaks in pieces and shatters everything; and like iron that crushes, that kingdom will break in pieces and crush all the others."

## Nebuchadnezzar's dream image – iron mixed with clay

In the next verses we learn specifically that the feet are of iron and the toes are part iron and part clay. This weakness amidst its strength occurs in the toes. The detail helps us accurately identify the final world empire. Jesus represented as the stone destroys this kingdom at His second coming at the battle of Armageddon.

Daniel 2:41-45 continues:

"Whereas you saw the feet and toes, partly of potter's clay and partly of iron, the kingdom shall be divided; yet the strength of the iron shall be in it, just as you saw the iron mixed with ceramic clay."

"And as the toes of the feet were partly of iron and partly of clay, so the kingdom shall be partly strong and partly fragile. As you saw iron mixed with ceramic clay, they will mingle with the seed of men; but they will not adhere to one another, just as iron does not mix with clay."

"And in the days of these kings the God of heaven will set up a kingdom which shall never be destroyed; and the kingdom shall not be left to other people; it shall break in pieces and consume all these kingdoms, and it shall stand forever."

"Inasmuch as you saw that the stone was cut out of the mountain without hands, and that it broke in pieces the iron, the bronze, the clay, the silver, and the gold—the great God has made known to the king what will come to pass after this. The dream is certain, and its interpretation is sure."

## Identity of the Beast of Revelation

The Beast of Revelation is the area that causes Bible Prophecy watchers the greatest disagreement.

They differ on the identity of the final world empire and how the Antichrist comes into power. Two views prevail. The one this author embraces is that the European Union is the final world empire—the beast of Revelation. The other view identifies the revived Islamic Caliphate, which became popular with the spread of Islam in our world, as being the last world empire. There are also those who combine both. They teach that the Beast is the revived Roman empire, with legs in the Middle East, which is not even a remote geopolitical possibility or foretold in Scripture.

There are also the conspiracy theorists who believe a conspiracy will bring about world rule and a revived empire. These cult beliefs have crept into Evangelical circles. Prophecy in the

Bible is clear that there is no conspiracy that brings the Antichrist or his government to power. The Antichrist is a deceiver. He is cunning and obtains his position through deceit. He enters his political seat—referred to as the seat of the Antichrist—through the empire's political process.

Concerning the Bible's accuracy, Daniel provides a view to empires that were yet future, and a final world empire. An unfolding sign of these end times is that we are geopolitically in what is called the age of empires, or a multipolar world. This world is governed by the EU, US, and the BRICs Russia, India, China, and Brazil.

## The European Union-The Final World Empire

The European Union is the final world empire: the revived Roman empire. At the time of the Tribulation, it will reign as the leading empire. Before the final signing of the Treaty of Rome that established the European Community in 1957, Paul-Henri Spaak, while gazing over the Roman Forum in Rome said, "I think that we have re-established the Roman Empire without a single shot being fired."

This is not the only time that a European Union politician has compared the evolving European Union to the Roman Empire. At the inception of the euro, it was pointed out that the Roman Empire also had its own currency.

## The ten king structure of the revived Roman Empire

The books of Daniel and the Revelation make it clear that within the final world empire are ten kings. These give their power or authority to the Beast. This currently mirrors the construct of the EU institutions and is enshrined in the EU treaties. The EU nations give their authority to a higher authority: the European Commission, which has a president.

It should be noted that the books of Daniel and the Revelation, during Empire ages, predicted modern politics. This includes the nation states which formed in the 1800's and 1900's and provide the 'ten kings' composition of the final world empire. In addition, it includes the rebirth of the nation of Israel.

# 8 THE MARK OF THE BEAST

Revelation 13 tells us that the Antichrist initiates the mark of the Beast, which is one of the most frightening forecasts in end times Bible Prophecy. The mark of the Beast is a mark that the Antichrist will make everyone take. Without it, people will not be able to buy or sell. The mark no doubt depicts life in a police state. Even more alarming, taking the mark guarantees one will go to hell. The issuing of the mark begins at the start of the Great Tribulation.

It is from the Revelation 13 passage that Bible Prophecy experts, decades ago, were able to gauge that the mark of the Beast was a future technology. They were correct on their speculations because years later we saw the arrival of mark of the Beast technologies that fits the Bible's description.

In examining the latest technologies, it is now clear why one will go to hell if they take the mark. The mark of the Beast will allow the Antichrist to mimic the Holy Trinity, and thus blaspheme the Holy Spirit. Moreover, whoever takes the mark will commit the unpardonable sin of blasphemy against the Holy Spirit. Therefore, the abomination of desolation is to be understood in a spiritual as well as physical dimension. The physical is the Antichrist's siege of Jerusalem and Israel.

**The Image of the Beast**

In addition to the mark of the Beast, we read about the image of the Beast. The image and mark are written about in Scripture together. Everyone must worship the image and also take the mark—which number is 666. This parallels with Nebuchadnezzar's 6 cubit tall, 6-cubit wide image that the Babylonians were to fall down and worship or face death. The False Prophet gives the image of the Beast life—but only with God's permission. He then makes sure everyone worships the image and takes the mark of the Beast.

## Decoding 666–The Number of the Beast

In this work I am providing an overview of the nuts and bolts of Bible Prophecy topics. For an extensive teaching on the mark of the Beast see my book, *Decoding 666, The Number of the Beast*. The book is not only an in-depth study, but also an up-to-date report on the status of technology that fits the mark of the Beast forecast.

# 9 THE WHORE OF BABYLON

The book of Revelation, Chapters 17 and 18, describe the Whore of Babylon. She is first introduced as the "Great Harlot who sits on many waters." The kings of the earth have committed fornication with her. The inhabitants were made drunk with the wine of her fornication. She sits on top of a scarlet beast filled with the names of blasphemy. It has seven heads and ten horns.

**Simply what does the Whore of Babylon of Revelation 17 & 18 represent?**

The Whore of Babylon represents false religion. These false religion beliefs seduce both men and women away from the truth and the one true God of the Bible.

The Beast represents the various world empires. These kings embraced the religion of their days. They also united with the gods and claimed to be the sons of the gods. Hence, they committed fornication with her by uniting with her. Wine represents teaching; therefore, the inhabitants become drunk with the wine or teachings from this union.

## The Whore of Babylon is described in Revelation 17 and 18

She has a name written on her forehead: Mystery Babylon the Great, the Mother of Harlots and of the Abominations of the Earth. She wears purple and scarlet. Additionally, she is decked in gold, precious stones and pearls. She holds a golden cup full of abominations and the filthiness of her fornication.

Each aspect of the Whore symbolizes spiritual deceptions. She also provides an overview of history while giving a forecast of what will come during the Tribulation. She represents both a religious and political dimension of the

Kingdom. Within her the nations also trade. Like Babylon, she is a commercial hub.

**The Whore sits on seven hills and the Bible refers to her as a city**

The seven hills are those of Rome. The city is Rome. There are many reasons why Rome is identified. For a more detailed and in-depth study see my book, *Whore of Babylon in Bible Prophecy: A Book of Revelation Mystery Revealed.*

**The Whore first appears in Zechariah Chapter 5**

The Whore of Babylon first appears as the woman in the basket in Zechariah 5. God names her Wickedness. Ancient Israel worshipped her. We read an account of this worship in Jeremiah 44.

**The Whore is drunk with the blood of the Saints**

A key to the Whore's identity is that she has martyred the Saints. In addition, she is also drunk with the blood of the Saints; this includes the past as well as continuing through the Tribulation. Christians will be martyred by political Babylon. Only at that time, the Antichrist replaces the Whore and sets himself up as the true religion. Even worse, he blasphemes the Holy Trinity.

## The Whore of Babylon influences the Beast of Revelation's formation

In Bible Prophecy, we see the Whore of Babylon's influence in the kingdom of the Beast. She plays a major role in the Beast of Revelation coming to power. Kings, leaders and statesmen embrace her. Hence, their policies reflects their union with her.

## The Beast of Revelation destroys the Great Harlot in Revelation 18

While the previous kingdoms embraced the Harlot and committed fornication with her, the Beast of Revelation carries her. Initially, she sits on top of the Beast as a queen. Especially relevant is the Beast and the ten kings are carrying her—signifying she has become a burden. The Beast ends up destroying her.

## How is the Great Harlot destroyed by the Beast?

The Beast strips her naked, makes her desolate, eats her flesh, and burns her with fire. In summary, the Beast will unleash persecution against her followers and take all of the church's possessions. The Antichrist will have a zero-tolerance policy toward all religion. This most likely occurs at the start of the Great Tribulation and continues until its end.

## Physical Babylon is Destroyed

After the destruction of the Whore, physical Babylon receives judgement as well. However, this most likely occurs at the end of the Tribulation—just prior to the battle of Armageddon. Based on the description in Scripture, it can occur via a nuclear bomb.

# 10 BOOK OF REVELATION

The final bowl judgements, which are the worst of the Revelation plagues, occur after the Antichrist and his regime martyr the last Christian on the earth. While the Tribulation Saints live through most of the Tribulation and die under the Antichrist's wrath, they are spared the horrific final plagues of the Revelation.

## The Book of Revelation–Judgements and Plagues

The book of Revelation's Judgments are issued by Jesus who opens the seven seals himself. From the seals, seven angels are given seven trumpets. Each trumpet sounds a judgement onto the earth. These seven angels sound trumpets, and the other angels pour plagues from bowls. These are referred to as the trumpet and bowl judgements.

## The Three Woes

The book of Revelation also relays the three woes, which happen along with the trumpet and bowl judgments.

These are the events that occur during the Tribulation and lead up to the battle of Armageddon. A mountain and island leveling earthquake occurs at the end of the battle. At the sounding of the seventh trumpet are the catastrophic events that lead to the destruction of the earth, the appearing of Christ in the clouds, the end of the world, and the proclamation: "It is Done."

## New Heaven and Earth

In chapters 21 and 22 of the book of Revelation we read of the new heaven and the new earth. The Revelation concludes with an invitation to all by Jesus to come to Him and Christ affirms—He is coming again.

## Book of Revelation—God's Throne

The book of Revelation contains 22 chapters. The opening verse of the book of Revelation begins; "The Revelation of Jesus Christ, which God gave Him to show His servants—things which must shortly take place. And He sent and signified it by His angel to His servant John." Jesus proceeds to give John his letter to the seven churches; this letter to the churches end with an invitation.

After the message to the churches, the vision of the Revelation Prophecy begins and is revealed from the very throne room of God. While we see glimpses of God's throne in Ezekiel, Isaiah and Daniel—Jesus gives the Revelation directly from God's throne where Jesus resides.

## Seriousness of the Revelation's Message

In conclusion, four details reveal the dire seriousness of the Revelation prophecy.

1. Jesus's seal on the book
2. Jesus's warning against any who would add or take away from its Words

3. The prophecy depicted from God's throne itself
4. Jesus's declaration that He is coming without delay

The book of Revelation—the last book of the Bible—exists as one of the Bible's most mysterious and frightening texts. It predicts the end of today's world.

## Jesus is Revelation's Author

Of all New Testament books, Jesus identifies Himself directly as this book's author. Jesus also places his seal at the end of the book of Revelation—along with an invitation. Revelation 22:16-17 reads:

"I, Jesus, have sent My angel to testify to you these things in the churches. I am the Root and the Offspring of David, the Bright and Morning Star."

And the Spirit and the bride say, "Come!" And let him who hears say, "Come!" And let him who thirsts come. Whoever desires, let him take the water of life freely.

## Revelation is the Only Bible Book That Comes with a Warning

Jesus's warning comes after His invitation and after placing His seal on the book. Jesus states in Revelation 22:18-19:

"For I testify to everyone who hears the words of the prophecy of this book: If anyone adds to these things, God will add to him the plagues that are written in this book; and if anyone takes away from the words of the book of this prophecy, God shall take away his part from the Book of Life, from the holy city, and from the things which are written in this book."

## Jesus concludes the Revelation with His Declaration, "I Come Quickly"

Four times in the book of Revelation Jesus states, "I come quickly." Tachy, the Greek word for quickly: means quickly, speedily, without delay.

It is this author's view that the books of Revelation and Daniel speak directly to the Tribulation saints. Jesus's declaration that He is coming quickly, without delay, will provide them comfort and hope during what they will endure through the Tribulation and Great Tribulation.

Revelation 22:20-21 concludes the book of Revelation and states:

"He who testifies to these things says, 'Surely I am coming quickly.'"

Amen. Even so, come, Lord Jesus!

The grace of our Lord Jesus Christ be with you all. Amen.

# 11 BIBLE PROPHECY NEWS

Bible Prophecy news unfolds in specific ways based on the nuts and bolt areas of end times Bible Prophecy. In addition to this news—looking at the signs of the times in society and nature—the geopolitical areas are as follow:

- EU in Bible Prophecy – Revived Roman Empire – final world empire
- Israel in Prophecy – Third Temple
- US in Bible Prophecy – US Decline –rise of EU
- Russia in Prophecy – Ezekiel 38

- Prophecy and Finance – decline of dollar – rise of euro-cashless payment systems
- Technology – mark of the Beast developments

## Be on guard against end time prophecy false teachings

There are many false teachings being disseminated in end times prophecy concerning both the Biblical predictions, and how current events line with the forecasts.

One of the greatest reasons for these errors is related to the Bible Prophecy teacher's analysis of the latest news and current events. Many lack journalistic standards and mistakenly rely on news headlines or conspiracy theories. Conspiracy theories become the easy way out of spending the hours it takes to effectively research world affairs and consult viable sources. These have also turned into cults within Evangelical circles.

Many who teach Bible Prophecy do not understand political science, foreign affairs, and the world of news or how it is obtained. Some of these Bible Prophecy teachers even end up twisting Bible Prophecy to conform to the headlines, and do not provide any kind of accurate picture of current affairs and Bible Prophecy. They also lack in-depth knowledge of the prophetic forecasts.

False teachings are a major problem in the world of end times prophecy news. Consequently, this is also why some of today's Bible Prophecy experts are not taken seriously by anyone in the know. For this reason, they are not consulted like the prophets of the Old Testament or Magi of the New Testament. For more, see my book *Myth and Lies: Satan's Attack on Bible Prophecy News* for God's standard.

## Unfolding Bible Prophecy News

Despite the many false prophets teaching errors, Bible Prophecy news is unfolding at an unprecedented rate. Never have we seen in such a short period of time Bible Prophecy unrolling before our very eyes. Now that you have the nuts and bolts of Bible Prophecy teachings, may God bless you further in your studies on this most exciting topic—and may you experience the power of the Word of God and the Lord Jesus Christ.

The Nuts and Bolts of Bible Prophecy

# ABOUT THE AUTHOR

Erika Grey, author, Bible scholar, commentator, journalist has been a born-again Christian for over 40 years. She has written numerous books on Bible Prophecy and made contributions in helping to decode the more difficult forecasts. She has spoken on numerous radio stations including Coast to Coast and interviewed high level policy makers.

This book is one of a series of short books by Erika Grey intended to be quick reads with important information. Be sure to check out Erika's other titles at www.erikagrey.com.

www.ingramcontent.com/pod-product-compliance
Lightning Source LLC
Chambersburg PA
CBHW020234170426
43201CB00007B/428